How Full Is Full?

Comparing Bodies of Water

Vic Parker

Heinemann
LIBRARY

Chicago, Illinois

www.heinemannraintree.com
Visit our website to find out
more information about
Heinemann-Raintree books.

To order:
☎ Phone 888-454-2279
💻 Visit www.heinemannraintree.com
to browse our catalog and order online.

Edited by Nancy Dickmann, Rebecca Rissman, and Sian Smith
Designed by Victoria Allen
Picture research by Hannah Taylor
Original illustrations © Capstone Global Library 2011
Original illustrations by Victoria Allen
Production by Victoria Fitzgerald
Originated by Capstone Global Library Ltd
Printed and bound in China by South China Printing
 Company Ltd

14 13 12
10 9 8 7 6 5 4 3

Library of Congress Cataloging-in-Publication Data
Parker, Victoria.
 How full is full?:comparing bodies of water / Vic Parker.
  p. cm.—(Measuring and comparing)
 Includes bibliographical references and index.
 ISBN 978-1-4329-3957-1 (hc)—ISBN 978-1-4329-3965-6
(pb) 1. Volume (Cubic content)—Juvenile literature. I. Title.
 QC104.P37 2011
  530.8'1—dc22   2010000927

Acknowledgments
The author and publisher are grateful to the following for
permission to reproduce copyright material: © Capstone
Publishers pp. **4**, **5**, **8**, **26**, **27** (Karon Dubke); Corbis pp. **7**
(Bo Zaunders), **12** (David Shopper), **22** (Tom Van Sant); Getty
Images p. **25** (Chris Sattlberger); istockphoto pp. **6** (© Timothy
Goodwin), **14** (© Fabien Courtitarat), **20** (© Arpad Benedek);
Photolibrary pp. **10** (Stephen Beaudet), **16** (Tips Italia/
Bildagentur RM), **18** (Britain on View); shutterstock pp. **24**
(© Sally Scott).

Photographs used to create silhouettes: istockphoto, bath
(© Brandi Powell); shutterstock, bucket (© Matthew Cole),
child (© Robert Adrian Hillman), fish (© stock09), swimmers
(© gaga), reeds (© Kaetana), boats (© sabri denic kizil).

Cover photograph of a courtyard with a fountain reproduced
with permission of Photolibrary (Garden Picture Library/
Andrea Jones).

Every effort has been made to contact copyright holders
of material reproduced in this book. Any omissions will
be rectified in subsequent printings if notice is given to
the publisher.

Contents

Words appearing in the text in bold, **like this,**
are explained in the glossary.

Measuring Capacity

A liquid is something runny, such as water or milk. Liquids can fill up containers. The total space for liquid inside a container is called its **capacity**.

Containers come in many different shapes and sizes.

Liquids are usually measured in pints (pt.), quarts (qt.), or gallons (gal.). Smaller amounts can be measured in cups.

To measure small amounts, we can use measuring cups like this.

What Is a Body of Water?

A body of water is any amount of water in one place. A body of water can be big, such as an ocean or a sea. A body of water can be small, such as a pond or a puddle.

A puddle is a small, shallow body of water.

We use bodies of water in many ways. You can swim in a swimming pool or a lake. Boats sail on rivers, lakes, and oceans. They carry people and **goods** from place to place.

A huge amount of our planet is covered with water, so boats can be a good way to travel.

A Glass of Water

Have you ever measured how much water a glass can hold? Compared to a spoon, it can hold a lot. But what can hold more water than a glass?

Drinking plenty of water can help you stay healthy.

A bucket can hold more than a glass of water. Most buckets hold over 3 gallons. It would take around 30 glasses to hold as much water as a full bucket.

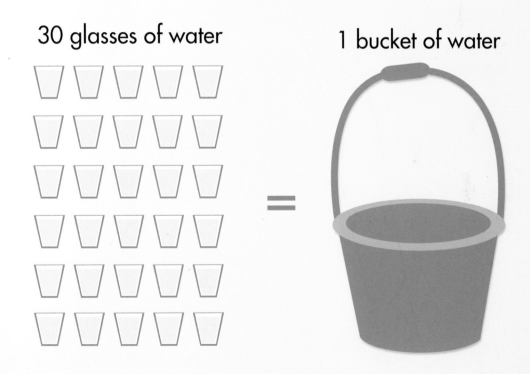

30 glasses of water = 1 bucket of water

What can hold more water than a bucket? ➡

A Bath

A bath can hold more than a bucket. Baths come in lots of different shapes and sizes. A bath with a person in it cannot hold as much water as when no one is in it.

Taking a bath can be a fun way to keep clean!

A regular-sized bath can hold about 53 gallons of water. If you tried to fill up a bath by using buckets of water, you would need over 16 full buckets.

16 buckets of water

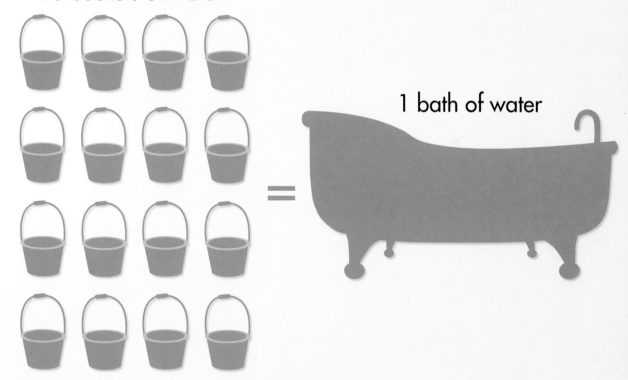

1 bath of water

What can hold more water than a bath? ➡

A Fish Pond

A pond in a garden can hold more water than a bath. Many people like having a small pond in their garden. Ponds are also found in parks.

A pond can be a home for fish.

Fish ponds can be different shapes and sizes. A small pond might hold about 1,585 gallons of water. This is as much water as about 30 baths.

30 baths of water

the water in 1 fish pond

=

What can hold more water than a fish pond? ➡

A Swimming Pool

A swimming pool can hold more than a fish pond. An Olympic-sized swimming pool can hold a huge amount of water —about 660,253 gallons!

Olympic-sized pools are often used for swimming races.

If you wanted to fill up an Olympic-sized swimming pool using fish ponds full of water, you would need about 416 full fish ponds.

the water in 1 Olympic swimming pool

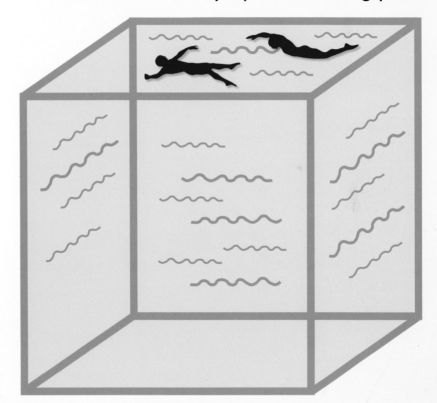

the water in
1 fish pond

**What can hold more water
than a swimming pool?** ➡

A Canal Lock

A canal lock can hold more than a swimming pool. Canals look like rivers, but they are built by people. A lock is a part of a canal that can be closed off by gates.

A lock can take boats down to a lower canal level, or raise them up to a higher canal level.

A canal lock must be big enough to hold a boat. Some of the biggest locks hold as much water as 40 full Olympic-sized swimming pools.

the water in 1 large canal lock

the water in 1 Olympic swimming pool

What can hold more water than a canal lock? ➡

A Reservoir

A **reservoir** can hold more than a **canal lock**.
A reservoir is a natural or human-made pool.
Most reservoirs are made when a **dam** is
built to block a river.

Reservoirs are built to hold water that can later be used in people's homes.

dam

Clywedog reservoir

Clywedog (pronounced "Cluw-ed-og") reservoir is a fairly small reservoir in the United Kingdom. Even so, you would need the water from about 500 large canal locks to fill the Clywedog reservoir.

the water in Clywedog reservoir

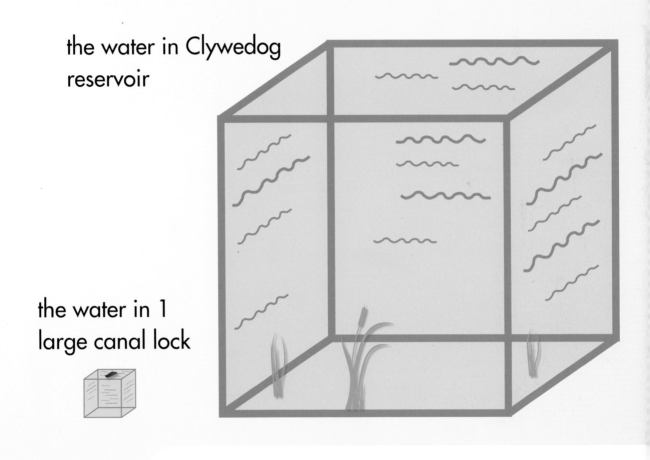

the water in 1 large canal lock

What can hold more water than a reservoir? ➡

A Lake

A lake can hold more than a **reservoir**. A lake is a large body of water that is surrounded by land on all sides. Lake Superior is one of the world's largest lakes.

Lake Superior lies between Canada and the United States.

Lake Superior is so enormous that in some places, you cannot see from one side of it to the other. It would take 242,000 Clywedog reservoirs to fill Lake Superior.

the water in Lake Superior

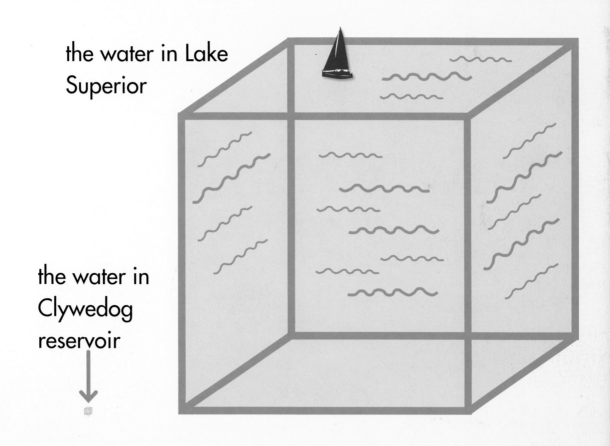

the water in Clywedog reservoir

What can hold more water than a lake?

A Sea

A sea can hold more than a lake. A sea is a body of moving water connected to a bigger ocean. The Mediterranean is a sea that feeds into the Atlantic Ocean.

The water in the Mediterranean Sea is salty, like the water in the ocean.

ATLANTIC OCEAN

Europe

Asia

MEDITERRANEAN SEA

Africa

The Mediterranean Sea lies between southern Europe, western Asia, and northern Africa. It would take more than 347 Lake Superiors to fill the Mediterranean Sea.

the water in the Mediterranean Sea

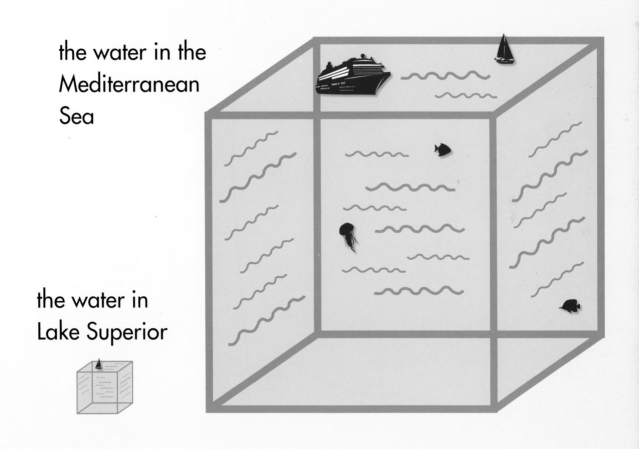

the water in Lake Superior

What can hold more water than a sea? ➡

An Ocean

An ocean is bigger than a sea. The largest ocean on Earth is the Pacific Ocean. It contains more than half of all the water on Earth.

The Pacific Ocean covers about one-third of Earth's surface.

It would take more than 160 Mediterranean Seas to fill the Pacific Ocean. That's more than three trillion, four hundred billion (3,400,000,000,000) baths!

The Pacific Ocean is so big that it can take several weeks to sail across it.

Measuring Activity

Things you will need: water, a 2-cup measuring cup, and containers of different shapes and sizes (see-through ones are best). For example: a cup, a shallow dish, a deep bowl, and a tall, thin vase.

1 Fill the measuring cup to the 1 cup mark.

2 Pour your water into one of the containers.

(3) Fill the measuring cup with 1 cup of
water and pour it into another container.

(4) Do the same until all of the containers have
1 cup of water in them.

Find out: Does it look as though there is the
same amount of water in each container?

Full Quiz and Facts

Measuring liquid

Small amounts are measured in cups.

Larger amounts are measured in pints (pt.), quarts (qt.), or gallons (gal.).

Remember

16 cups = 1 gallon (gal.)

Quiz

1. What unit would you use to measure the amount of water in a wading pool?

   a) cups   b) gallons

2. What unit would you use to measure the amount of water in a vase of flowers?

   a) cups   b) gallons

Answers: 1 = b   2 = a

Full Facts

- The five "Great Lakes" of North America are Lake Superior, Lake Huron, Lake Michigan, Lake Erie, and Lake Ontario. Together they form the largest lake group in the world.

- The Caspian Sea is the world's largest lake.

- There are five oceans on Earth. The largest ocean is the Pacific Ocean.

- Very large amounts of water are measured in **cubic** miles. Imagine a huge cube made of water. If all the sides of the cube were 1 mile long, that would be 1 cubic mile of water.

- Lake Nasser is a huge **reservoir** that was created when the Aswan **Dam** was built across the Nile River. It holds 32 cubic miles of water.

- There are a whopping eighty-five million and one hundred thousand (85,100,000) cubic miles of water in the Atlantic Ocean.

Glossary

canal human-made body of water, similar to a river

capacity maximum amount that something will hold. A container's capacity is the biggest amount that the container can hold.

cubic shaped like a cube. Most dice are shaped like cubes. Every side on a cube is the same length.

dam strong wall that is built across a river or stream to trap water

goods things that people buy or sell, such as food or clothes

lock part of a canal that can be closed off by gates. Locks are used to move ships up or down to different levels of the canal.

reservoir large lake used to hold water that can later be used in people's homes and businesses. Natural lakes are sometimes made into reservoirs or reservoirs are built by people.

Find Out More

Books

Ganeri, Anita. *I Wonder Why the Sea Is Salty and Other Questions About the Ocean.* New York: Kingfisher, 2009.

Guillain, Charlotte. *Investigate: Water.* Chicago: Heinemann Library, 2009.

Hughes, Monica. *What Is an Ocean? (The World Around Us series)* Chicago: Heinemann Library, 2005.

Web Sites

http://pbskids.org/cyberchase/games/liquidvolume/liquidvolume.html

Try this fun game, where you have to fill a container using a combination of different sized pots in as few attempts as possible.

www.cdfa.ca.gov/dms/kidspage/KidsIndex.htm

Find out more about units of measurement through the facts and activities offered on this website.

Index